A Robbie Reader

Syd Hoff

Josepha Sherman

Mitchell Lane
PUBLISHERS

P.O. Box 196
Hockessin, Delaware 19707
Visit us on the web: www.mitchelllane.com
Comments? email us: mitchelllane@mitchelllane.com

Printing   1   2   3   4   5   6   7   8   9

A Robbie Reader

Albert Einstein	Alex Rodriguez	Barbara Park
Charles Schulz	Dale Earnhardt Jr.	Donovan McNabb
Dr. Seuss	Henry Ford	Hilary Duff
Jamie Lynn Spears	Johnny Gruelle	LeBron James
Mia Hamm	Philo T. Farnsworth	Robert Goddard
Shaquille O'Neal	The Story of Harley-Davidson	**Syd Hoff**
Thomas Edison	Tony Hawk	

Library of Congress Cataloging-in-Publication Data
Sherman, Josepha.
    Syd Hoff / by Josepha Sherman.
        p. cm. — (A robbie reader)
    Includes bibliographical references and index.
    ISBN 1-58415-357-1 (library bound)
    1. Hoff, Syd, 1912— Juvenile literature. 2. Authors, American — 20th century—
Biography — Juvenile literature. 3. Cartoonists — United States — Biography —
Juvenile literature. 4. Children's stories — Authorship — Juvenile literature. I. Title.
II. Series.
    PS3558.O344424Z86 2005
    741.5′092 — dc22
                                        2004030538

ABOUT THE AUTHOR: Josepha Sherman is a professional fantasy and science fiction writer, a *Star Trek* novelist, a children's writer, and a nonfiction writer with over 60 books in print and over 150 short stories. She is also a professional folklorist and editor. In addition, she is a native New Yorker, has a degree in archaeology, loves to tinker with computers, follows the NY Mets ("wait till next year!"), and is a horse whisperer who has had a new foal fall asleep on her foot!

PHOTO CREDITS: All photographs courtesy of Syd Hoff's family.
ACKNOWLEDGMENTS: This story has been approved by the family of Syd Hoff.

TABLE OF CONTENTS

This picture of Syd Hoff was taken when he was a young man.

"It Was All Like a Dream"

In the 1920s, Syd Hoff wasn't yet a great cartoonist. He wasn't yet a famous writer. Syd Hoff was still a high school student. Syd did like to draw and he took art classes at school. He had liked to draw since he was a little boy.

One day, though, there was a guest speaker at his high school. When Syd heard who it was, he grew very excited. The guest was Milt Gross who was a very famous **cartoonist**.

CHAPTER ONE

Syd at his 50th high school reunion. When it was his turn to speak, he entertained everyone by drawing cartoons.

Milt Gross picked Syd out of the audience (AW-dee-yens). He asked Syd to come up on stage with him and do some illustrations (ill-us-TRAY-shuns). It wasn't easy to draw in front of the whole school because Syd was nervous, but he did his best.

When he was finished, Syd stepped back. He wasn't sure what would happen next.

Milt Gross looked at the drawings. Then he hugged Syd. "Kid, someday you'll be a great cartoonist!" he shouted.

He drew a sketch for Syd to keep. Syd was almost too amazed to move. A great cartoonist liked his work. A great cartoonist thought that he, too, would be great. Syd wrote about the day: "It was all like a dream."

It was a dream that was going to come true.

Here is a picture of Syd's parents, Mary and Ben. We don't know for sure when this photo was taken. But his parents look very happy together.

"An Artist"

Syd Hoff was born on September 4, 1912, in New York City. His parents were also from New York. Their names were Ben and Mary Hoffberg. Ben Hoffberg was a salesman. Syd had an older brother Danny and a younger sister Dorothy.

Syd said about himself, "I suppose I was born three years after the date of my birth." He meant that when he was three years old, something exciting sparked his life. His family took a **subway** ride. Syd drew a picture of the **subway conductor**. His mother cried, "Sydney is an artist."

Syd loved the cartoons in his father's magazines. They were funny. He liked the way the cartoons were drawn, too. Syd started drawing his own cartoons. Soon, he began writing jokes to go with his cartoons.

When Syd was fifteen, his friends and family knew he was an artist. He attended

This is a family photo. Syd is on the far left, and his wife, Dutch, is on the far right. Between them are his parents, Ben and Mary.

Morris High School, but Syd wasn't a very good student. Syd left high school before **graduation** (grad-oo-AY-shun) against the advice of his family and teachers. But fifty-two years later, Syd would receive an **honorary** high school diploma from the Board of Education.

Syd's brother Danny encouraged him to study art. So Syd went to art school. He entered the National Academy of Design in New York. There, he studied for three years with great artists. Syd was sure that he was going to be a painter.

His teachers didn't agree. They said his work was too funny. When he was eighteen, Syd sold a **cartoon** to *The New Yorker,* a famous magazine. "The die was cast," he said. "I was a cartoonist."

Syd and his wife, Dutch, pose for the camera. They look like a happy couple.

Cartoonist

At first, Syd didn't know he would write books. After he sold that first cartoon, he drew others. Soon he was a cartoonist for *The New Yorker* and other leading magazines and newspapers.

When he was twenty-five, Syd fell in love with a young woman named Dora Berman. Dora's nickname was Dutch. Dutch was a talented piano player. Syd and Dutch were married in 1937. They had two daughters, Susan and Bonnie. Syd loved to read stories to his daughters.

In 1939, William Randolph Hearst (the owner of many newspapers) heard about Syd. Mr. Hearst wanted Syd to write a **comic strip** for his newspaper. So, Syd created a **daily** comic strip that was about a little girl named Tuffy who did funny things. Every day, the strip told a new story. This comic strip ran for ten years. It was printed in about eight hundred newspapers.

While he was working on *Tuffy,* Syd decided to write a book for children. The book was called *Muscles and Brains.* It was published in 1940. The book did not sell very well, so Syd went back to doing cartoons for a while. He published a book of his cartoons in 1944. It was called *Feeling No Pain.*

Syd also drew illustrations for advertisements. His pictures helped sell many different products, from cars to coffee. The money he earned helped pay the bills.

Dutch and daughter Susan. Dutch is happy to show off her new baby. But Susan doesn't look so sure about the whole thing.

Dutch and Syd with their daughters Susan and Bonnie.

Author

In 1954, Syd wrote another book for children. It was called *Eight Little Artists.* In 1955, he wrote *Patty's Pet.* Neither book made him famous.

One year Susan injured her hip. She had to spend a lot of time in bed. Syd wanted to make Susan feel better. So, one day he drew a dinosaur with a boy on its back. The boy was supposed to be Danny, Syd's brother. Susan exclaimed, "That's Danny and the Dinosaur!" So Syd went on to write a story called *Danny and the Dinosaur.* In the story, Danny wants to play with the dinosaurs in a museum. One dinosaur likes the idea. Danny goes for a ride on its back. He and his friends even play hide-and-seek with the dinosaur. At the end of the day, the dinosaur goes home to the museum. Danny thinks about what a wonderful day he had.

Syd with daughter Bonnie. Syd loved being a father. That love helped him write such good books for children.

Susan got better. Syd published *Danny and the Dinosaur.* It was a big hit. The book is still in print today. It has sold over ten million copies. This book made Syd a famous author.

Syd kept on writing and illustrating. He wrote all kinds of books. He wrote **picture books**, which are almost all pictures, with very few words. He wrote **easy readers**, which are books for beginning readers. He illustrated books by other authors, too. In 1967, he wrote novels, such as *Irving and Me. The New York Times* said it was one the year's ten best books for children.

One of the best things about Syd Hoff's books is that his characters are always likable. The books are funny. The pictures, which are also funny, help tell the story. The story might be about a child and an animal who make friends. Or the story might be about a child or an animal who help a team win. One of his books, *Sammy*

This picture was taken when Syd traveled to Japan in 1962. The dog probably wasn't his. But it was definitely a friendly visitor.

the Seal, is about a seal who goes to school.

It was important to Syd that kids learn how to read. Many children have enjoyed reading his books.

Syd spoke to many groups of school children. Here he is showing them how he did his drawings. The colorful banner shows how happy everyone was to have him visit them.

Here is Syd at work. Wearing a colorful shirt, he is drawing a picture. Maybe it's for one of his books.

Author *and* Cartoonist

While he wrote books, Syd kept working as a cartoonist. From 1958 to 1977, he drew a cartoon series called *Laugh It Off*. This cartoon was featured in *The New Yorker*. He also wrote textbooks. One was called *Learning to Cartoon*. That book was about how to become a cartoonist. Syd also starred on a TV show called *Tales of Hoff*. It ran during the 1950s. In each **episode**, Syd told a story and drew cartoons.

Syd and his wife, Dutch, were very happy together. They both liked the warm weather, so they moved to Miami Beach, Florida.

After they moved, Syd would often go swimming in the ocean. He also enjoyed

Happy birthday, Syd! That silly hat is made of ribbons and paper. It came from the wrappings around his presents.

jogging and riding his bike. He was a very athletic person.

Syd's daughter, Susan, had children of her own. She had a boy and a girl. Syd loved having grandchildren. He also loved teaching children about drawing. Syd said, "I traveled all over the country, meeting

Syd poses happily with family. On the left is his sister, Dorothy Ross. On the right is her daughter, Carol, Syd's niece.

young people and giving them pointers in the art of cartooning."

One time Syd and Dutch traveled to Spain with Syd's sister Dorothy and her husband Dan. They were at a restaurant

Smile for the camera! Syd is with his sister and wife. On the left is Dorothy and on the right is Dutch.

and Syd wanted smoked salmon. Syd couldn't speak Spanish and the waiter couldn't speak English. Syd really wanted to eat smoked salmon, so he drew a picture of a salmon smoking a pipe. Then the waiter knew that Syd wanted smoked salmon and when it arrived for dinner Syd was happy.

In 1994, Dutch Hoff died. Syd was very sad. He had loved his wife very much.

Syd kept writing and illustrating, however. His last book was *Danny and the Dinosaur Go to Camp.* It was published in 1996.

On May 12, 2004, Syd Hoff died in Miami Beach, Florida. He was ninety-one years old.

Syd Hoff drew thousands of cartoons. He wrote or illustrated over two hundred books. His cartoons and books have made millions of people smile.

1912	Sydney Hoff is born on September 4 in New York City.
1927	Syd attends New York's National Academy of Design.
1928	Syd sells his first cartoon, to *The New Yorker*
1937	Syd marries Dutch (Dora) Berman.
1939–1949	Syd writes and draws the *Tuffy* comic strip.
1940	Syd publishes his first book, *Muscles and Brains.*
1958	Syd publishes *Danny and the Dinosaur.*
1958–1977	Syd writes a single-panel comic series called *Laugh It Off.*
1958–1996	Syd publishes over two hundred books for all ages.
1994	Dutch (Dora) Hoff dies.
2004	Syd Hoff dies on May 12.

Arturo's Baton

Barney's Horse

Captain Cat

Chester

Danny and the Dinosaur

Danny and the Dinosaur Go to Camp

Duncan the Dancing Duck

Happy Birthday, Danny and the Dinosaur!

Grizzwold

The Horse in Harry's Room

Julius

Learning to Cartoon

Mrs. Brice's Mice

Morris Goes to School

Oliver

Sammy the Seal

Stanley

Who Will Be My Friends?

cartoon (CAR-toon)—a funny drawing, often with a caption.

cartoonist (CAR-toon-ist)— someone who draws cartoons.

comic strip (KAH-mik-strip)—a row of cartoons telling a story or part of a story.

daily (DAY-lee)—printed every day or every weekday.

easy readers (e-Z REE-ders)—books for beginning readers.

episode (EH-peh-sode)—one part of a series.

graduation (grah-jeh-WAY-shun)—the completion of high school.

honorary (ON-or-airy)—an award given without fulfillment of the usual requirements.

novel (NAH-vul)—a long story that is printed without pictures.

picture book (PIK-shur buk)—a book that is mostly pictures, with very few words.

subway (SUHB-way)—a railroad that runs underground.

subway conductor (SUBH-way kon-DUK-tor)—one of the people who make sure that a subway train runs safely.

While there are no other books about Syd Hoff for children, maybe you'll enjoy having an adult read to you.

Books

Berger, Laura Standley, ed. *Twentieth-Century Children's Writers.* Detroit and London: St. James Press, 1995.

De Montreville, Doris, and Donna Hill. *Third Book of Junior Authors.* New York: The H. Wilson Company, 1972.

Newspaper and Magazine Articles

McMahon, Judith. "Review of *Danny and the Dinosaur,*" *School Library Journal,* 37, no. 2, February 1991, p. 53.

Nash, Eric P. "Syd Hoff, 91, Who Illustrated a Boy's Ride on a Dinosaur," obituary, *New York Times,* May 17, 2004.

INDEX